EMMANUEL JOSEPH

The Green Runway, Redefining Fashion
Through Ecology and Ethical Choices

Copyright © 2025 by Emmanuel Joseph

All rights reserved. No part of this publication may be reproduced, stored or transmitted in any form or by any means, electronic, mechanical, photocopying, recording, scanning, or otherwise without written permission from the publisher. It is illegal to copy this book, post it to a website, or distribute it by any other means without permission.

First edition

*This book was professionally typeset on Reedsy.
Find out more at reedsy.com*

Contents

1	Chapter 1: The Dawn of Ethical Fashion	1
2	Chapter 2: The Environmental Impact of Fast Fashion	3
3	Chapter 3: The Rise of Eco-Fashion	5
4	Chapter 4: Ethical Choices in Fashion Production	7
5	Chapter 5: Green Innovations in Fabric	9
6	Chapter 6: Sustainable Fashion Designers	11
7	Chapter 7: Consumer Awareness and Responsibility	13
8	Chapter 8: The Role of Technology	15
9	Chapter 9: Second-Hand and Upcycled Fashion	17
10	Chapter 10: The Circular Economy in Fashion	19
11	Chapter 11: Fashion Activism	21
12	Chapter 12: Ethical Fashion on a Budget	22
13	Chapter 13: The Impact of Fast Fashion on Developing...	23
14	Chapter 14: Sustainable Fashion Events and Collaborations	25
15	Chapter 15: The Future of Fashion: Predictions and...	27
16	Chapter 16: Personal Stories of Transformation	29
17	Chapter 17: Call to Action: Redefining Our Fashion Choices	31

1

Chapter 1: The Dawn of Ethical Fashion

The Birth of Fashion

Fashion has always been a reflection of society, culture, and personal expression. In ancient times, clothing was crafted with care and skill, often by hand, and tailored to fit the individual. Garments were made to last, and the materials used were sourced locally and sustainably. This period can be seen as the golden age of fashion, where quality and craftsmanship were paramount, and the environmental impact was minimal.

Industrialization and Mass Production

However, the advent of industrialization in the 18th and 19th centuries brought significant changes to the fashion industry. The invention of the sewing machine and the rise of factories revolutionized clothing production. Mass production became the norm, allowing for faster and cheaper production of garments. While this democratized fashion and made it accessible to the masses, it also marked the beginning of a disconnect between fashion and ethical practices.

The Rise of Fast Fashion

Fast forward to the late 20th century, and the concept of fast fashion emerged. Brands began to produce clothing at an unprecedented rate, introducing new collections multiple times a year to keep up with the latest trends. This shift not only led to a decline in garment quality but also had severe environmental and ethical repercussions. The demand for cheap, disposable fashion fueled exploitative labor practices and contributed to massive environmental degradation.

A Call for Change

Despite the challenges, the early 21st century has seen a growing awareness of the need for change within the fashion industry. Consumers, designers, and activists are increasingly advocating for ethical fashion practices that prioritize sustainability and human rights. The dawn of ethical fashion represents a return to the values of craftsmanship, quality, and environmental stewardship, setting the stage for a new era in fashion.

2

Chapter 2: The Environmental Impact of Fast Fashion

Uncovering the Damage

Fast fashion, characterized by its rapid production cycle and low-cost garments, has become a major contributor to environmental harm. Factories producing fast fashion garments often rely on cheap synthetic materials like polyester, which are derived from fossil fuels. These materials not only contribute to carbon emissions during production but also shed microplastics when washed, polluting our oceans.

Waste Generation and Landfills

The fast fashion model encourages frequent purchasing and disposal of clothing, leading to enormous waste. In many cases, discarded garments end up in landfills where they take hundreds of years to decompose. This chapter details the staggering amount of waste generated by the fashion industry and the long-term environmental consequences.

Water Pollution and Consumption

The fashion industry is one of the largest consumers of water globally. From growing cotton to dyeing fabrics, water is a crucial resource. Unfortunately, the industry is also a major polluter of water bodies due to the discharge of toxic chemicals from dyeing processes. We explore the detrimental effects on aquatic ecosystems and the scarcity of clean water in affected regions.

The Hidden Cost of Cheap Clothing

Cheap clothing comes at a high environmental cost. The production of low-cost garments often involves practices that are harmful to the environment and exploitative to workers. This chapter sheds light on the hidden costs of fast fashion, urging readers to consider the true price of their clothing choices.

3

Chapter 3: The Rise of Eco-Fashion

Pioneers of Sustainability

The eco-fashion movement has gained momentum thanks to visionary pioneers who recognized the need for change. These trailblazers introduced sustainable practices long before they became mainstream, using recycled materials and promoting ethical production. Their stories inspire a new generation of designers and consumers.

Innovative Materials and Processes

Eco-fashion is characterized by the use of innovative materials such as organic cotton, hemp, and bamboo. These materials are grown and processed with minimal environmental impact. Additionally, eco-friendly dyeing techniques and water-efficient production processes have been developed to reduce pollution and conserve resources.

The Role of Certifications

Certifications play a crucial role in ensuring the authenticity of eco-fashion claims. Organizations like the Global Organic Textile Standard (GOTS) and Fair Trade International set stringent criteria for sustainable and ethical practices. This chapter explores the significance of certifications and how they help consumers make informed choices.

Consumer Demand for Eco-Fashion

As awareness of environmental issues grows, so does consumer demand for eco-friendly fashion. This chapter examines the shift in consumer behavior and the increasing preference for sustainable brands. We also highlight the efforts of companies that are leading the way in eco-fashion.

4

Chapter 4: Ethical Choices in Fashion Production

The Dark Side of Fashion

The fashion supply chain is often marred by unethical practices, including exploitative labor, poor working conditions, and insufficient wages. This chapter delves into the harsh realities faced by garment workers, particularly in developing countries where labor laws are lax.

Fair Trade and Ethical Brands

Fair Trade initiatives and ethical brands are working to address these issues by ensuring fair wages, safe working conditions, and respect for workers' rights. We profile several brands that have committed to ethical production and explore the impact of fair trade on communities.

Transparency in the Supply Chain

Transparency is key to fostering trust and accountability in the fashion industry. This chapter discusses the importance of supply chain transparency and the steps brands are taking to disclose their production practices. We also highlight the role of technology, such as blockchain, in enhancing transparency.

Empowering Consumers

Consumers have the power to drive change through their purchasing decisions. This chapter offers practical tips on how to support ethical fashion, from researching brands to asking questions about production practices. Empowered consumers can hold brands accountable and advocate for better standards.

5

Chapter 5: Green Innovations in Fabric

The Evolution of Fabrics

Fabrics have evolved significantly, with innovations aimed at reducing environmental impact. This chapter explores the development of sustainable fabrics, including organic cotton, hemp, bamboo, and recycled polyester. Each material's benefits and challenges are examined in detail.

Biodegradable and Recycled Materials

Biodegradable materials, such as Tencel and organic hemp, are designed to decompose naturally without harming the environment. Recycled materials, like polyester made from plastic bottles, reduce waste and conserve resources. We delve into the science behind these materials and their potential to transform the fashion industry.

Technological Advancements

Technology is playing a crucial role in developing sustainable fabrics. From lab-grown leather to bio-fabrication, innovative technologies are pushing the boundaries of what's possible in eco-friendly fashion. This chapter highlights some of the most promising advancements and their implications for the future.

The Impact on Fashion Design

Sustainable fabrics are not just environmentally friendly; they also inspire creativity and innovation in fashion design. We explore how designers are using these materials to create beautiful, functional, and sustainable garments that challenge conventional fashion norms.

6

Chapter 6: Sustainable Fashion Designers

Trailblazers of Sustainability

Sustainable fashion designers are at the forefront of the movement, redefining what it means to create fashion responsibly. This chapter profiles several trailblazing designers who prioritize sustainability in their collections. Their journeys, philosophies, and contributions to eco-fashion are celebrated.

Design Philosophy and Practices

Sustainable fashion goes beyond materials; it's about rethinking the entire design process. We explore the design philosophies and practices of leading sustainable designers, from zero-waste patterns to eco-friendly dyeing techniques. Their commitment to reducing environmental impact is inspiring a new generation of creators.

Collaborations and Partnerships

Collaborations between designers, brands, and organizations are driving innovation in sustainable fashion. This chapter highlights successful partnerships that have resulted in groundbreaking collections and initiatives. These collaborations demonstrate the power of collective effort in achieving sustainability goals.

Inspiring the Next Generation

Sustainable fashion designers are not just creating garments; they're shaping the future of the industry. By mentoring young designers and advocating for sustainable practices, they are inspiring the next generation to prioritize ethics and ecology in their work.

7

Chapter 7: Consumer Awareness and Responsibility

The Power of Informed Choices

Consumers play a crucial role in driving demand for sustainable fashion. This chapter discusses the importance of being informed and making conscious choices. We provide practical tips on how to research brands, read labels, and support ethical fashion.

Understanding Labels and Certifications

Labels and certifications can be confusing, but they are essential for identifying sustainable products. We break down the most common certifications, such as Fair Trade, GOTS, and OEKO-TEX, and explain what they mean. This knowledge empowers consumers to make eco-friendly purchases.

The Impact of Consumer Behavior

Consumer behavior has a significant impact on the fashion industry. From boycotting unethical brands to supporting sustainable initiatives, we explore how individual actions can collectively drive change. Real-life examples of consumer-driven movements are highlighted to illustrate the power of collective effort.

Building a Sustainable Wardrobe

Building a sustainable wardrobe is a journey, not a destination. This chapter offers practical advice on how to curate a wardrobe that reflects your values.

Tips include investing in quality pieces, embracing second-hand fashion, and adopting a minimalist approach to consumption.

8

Chapter 8: The Role of Technology

Technological Advancements in Fashion

Technology is revolutionizing the fashion industry, offering innovative solutions to sustainability challenges. This chapter explores advancements like 3D printing, AI in design, and blockchain for transparency. These technologies promise a future where fashion and technology coalesce to reduce waste and improve accountability.

3D Printing and Sustainable Design

3D printing allows for precise, on-demand production, reducing waste and excess inventory. This chapter delves into how designers are using 3D printing to create customized, sustainable garments. The potential for zero-waste fashion is also discussed.

Artificial Intelligence in Fashion

AI is transforming the way fashion is designed, produced, and consumed. From trend forecasting to personalized shopping experiences, AI can optimize every aspect of the fashion industry. We explore the benefits of AI in promoting sustainability and reducing environmental impact.

Blockchain for Transparency

Blockchain technology offers a new level of transparency in the fashion supply chain. By providing a secure and immutable record of every step in the production process, blockchain can ensure accountability and authenticity. This chapter highlights how blockchain is being used to enhance transparency and build consumer trust.

9

Chapter 9: Second-Hand and Upcycled Fashion

The Appeal of Second-Hand Fashion

Second-hand fashion is experiencing a renaissance, driven by environmental and economic considerations. This chapter explores the growing popularity of thrift stores, vintage shops, and online resale platforms. We discuss the benefits of buying second-hand and how it contributes to a more sustainable fashion industry.

The Art of Upcycling

Upcycling is the creative process of transforming old or discarded items into new, functional pieces. This chapter highlights the innovative ways designers and DIY enthusiasts are upcycling garments and accessories. We share inspiring stories of upcycled fashion projects that have made a significant impact.

Circular Fashion Economy

The concept of a circular fashion economy emphasizes keeping products in use for as long as possible. This chapter discusses how second-hand and upcycled fashion contribute to a circular economy by extending the life of garments and reducing waste.

Community and Culture of Thrifting

Thrifting is more than just shopping; it's a community-driven movement.

We explore the cultural and social aspects of thrifting, from local thrift store events to online communities that celebrate second-hand fashion. The sense of community and shared values makes thrifting a rewarding and enjoyable experience.

10

Chapter 10: The Circular Economy in Fashion

Principles of a Circular Economy

A circular economy aims to eliminate waste and continuously use resources. This chapter explains the principles of a circular economy and how they can be applied to the fashion industry. We discuss the benefits of designing for longevity, promoting recycling initiatives, and implementing closed-loop systems.

Designing for Longevity

Designing garments that are built to last is a key aspect of a circular economy. This chapter delves into the importance of quality materials, timeless designs, and craftsmanship. We highlight brands that focus on durability and share tips for consumers to identify well-made clothing.

Recycling Initiatives

Recycling is a cornerstone of the circular economy. This chapter explores various recycling initiatives within the fashion industry, from textile recycling programs to innovations in fabric recycling technology. We discuss the challenges and opportunities associated with recycling garments.

Closed-Loop Systems

A closed-loop system ensures that materials are continually reused, minimizing waste. This chapter examines how the fashion industry can implement closed-loop systems, from take-back programs to upcycling initiatives. We highlight successful examples and the potential for widespread adoption.

11

Chapter 11: Fashion Activism

The Power of Activism

Activism has played a crucial role in pushing the fashion industry towards sustainability. This chapter highlights influential activists, movements, and campaigns that have successfully advocated for ethical and ecological reforms in fashion.

Grassroots Movements

Grassroots movements have been instrumental in raising awareness and driving change. This chapter explores the impact of local initiatives, community organizations, and social media campaigns. We share inspiring stories of individuals and groups making a difference.

High-Profile Advocates

High-profile advocates, including celebrities and designers, have used their platforms to promote sustainable fashion. This chapter profiles several notable figures who have championed eco-friendly practices and influenced public opinion. Their efforts have brought sustainability to the forefront of the fashion industry.

The Role of Education

Education is key to fostering a culture of sustainability. This chapter discusses the importance of incorporating sustainability into fashion education and training programs. We highlight institutions and courses that are leading the way in educating the next generation of designers and consumers.

12

Chapter 12: Ethical Fashion on a Budget

Affordable Sustainable Fashion

Sustainable fashion doesn't have to be expensive. This chapter offers practical advice on how to build an eco-friendly wardrobe without breaking the bank. Tips include shopping second-hand, supporting local artisans, and investing in quality over quantity.

Thrifting and Vintage Shopping

Thrifting and vintage shopping are cost-effective ways to embrace sustainable fashion. This chapter explores the benefits of buying second-hand and provides tips for finding hidden gems in thrift stores and vintage shops. We also discuss online platforms that make thrifting accessible to everyone.

DIY and Upcycling

DIY projects and upcycling are creative ways to revamp old clothing. This chapter offers ideas and tutorials for transforming garments and accessories into new, stylish pieces. We share stories of individuals who have embraced DIY fashion and the positive impact it has on the environment.

Supporting Local Artisans

Supporting local artisans and small businesses is a great way to find affordable, sustainable fashion. This chapter highlights the benefits of buying handmade and locally produced items. We profile artisans who prioritize eco-friendly practices and offer unique, high-quality products.

13

Chapter 13: The Impact of Fast Fashion on Developing Countries

Socio-Economic Impact

Fast fashion's repercussions extend globally, particularly affecting developing nations. This chapter explores the socio-economic impact of fast fashion, including job creation and economic dependency. We discuss the challenges faced by garment workers and the efforts to improve working conditions.

Environmental Consequences

The environmental impact of fast fashion is felt acutely in developing countries. This chapter examines the pollution and resource depletion caused by garment production. We highlight the efforts of local communities and organizations to mitigate these effects and promote sustainable practices.

Human Rights and Labor Practices

Exploitation of labor is a significant issue in the fast fashion industry. This chapter delves into the human rights abuses faced by garment workers, including low wages, unsafe working conditions, and lack of labor protections. We discuss the importance of advocating for fair labor practices and supporting ethical brands.

Empowering Communities

Empowering communities to embrace sustainable practices can lead to positive change. This chapter explores initiatives that provide education, resources, and support to garment workers and their communities. We share success stories of programs that have improved livelihoods and promoted environmental stewardship.

14

Chapter 14: Sustainable Fashion Events and Collaborations

Fashion Weeks and Sustainable Runways
　　Fashion weeks and sustainable runways are crucial for spreading awareness and showcasing eco-friendly designs. This chapter highlights notable events that have successfully promoted sustainable fashion on a global stage. We discuss the impact of these events on the industry and consumer behavior.

Designer and Brand Collaborations
Collaborations between designers and brands can drive innovation and promote sustainability. This chapter profiles successful partnerships that have resulted in groundbreaking collections and initiatives. We explore how these collaborations benefit both the environment and the fashion industry.

Community and Industry Events
Local and industry events play a vital role in fostering a culture of sustainability. This chapter explores the impact of community-driven initiatives, workshops, and conferences. We highlight events that have brought together designers, consumers, and stakeholders to discuss and promote sustainable fashion.

Awards and Recognition
Awards and recognition can incentivize and celebrate sustainability in

fashion. This chapter discusses notable awards that honor eco-friendly practices and innovative designs. We profile recipients who have made significant contributions to sustainable fashion.

15

Chapter 15: The Future of Fashion: Predictions and Possibilities

Emerging Trends

The future of fashion is shaped by emerging trends that prioritize sustainability. This chapter explores potential trends, including slow fashion, minimalism, and digital fashion. We discuss how these trends can reshape the industry and promote a more sustainable future.

Technological Advancements

Technology will continue to play a crucial role in the future of fashion. This chapter highlights advancements such as smart textiles, virtual fashion shows, and AI-driven design. We explore the potential of these technologies to reduce waste, improve efficiency, and enhance sustainability.

Societal Shifts

Societal attitudes towards fashion are changing, with a growing emphasis on sustainability and ethical practices. This chapter examines the cultural and generational shifts that are driving these changes. We discuss the potential for a more conscious and responsible fashion industry.

Collaborative Efforts

The future of sustainable fashion relies on collaboration between designers, brands, consumers, and policymakers. This chapter explores the importance of collective effort in achieving sustainability goals. We highlight successful collaborations and discuss how they can serve as models for future initiatives.

16

Chapter 16: Personal Stories of Transformation

Embracing Sustainable Fashion
Real-life stories of individuals who have embraced sustainable fashion practices offer inspiration and insight. This chapter shares narratives of people who have made eco-conscious choices and the positive impact it has had on their lives and the environment.

Overcoming Challenges
Transitioning to sustainable fashion can come with challenges. This chapter explores the obstacles individuals have faced and how they have overcome them. We highlight the resilience and determination required to make lasting changes.

Community and Support
Support from family, friends, and communities can make the journey towards sustainable fashion more manageable. This chapter discusses the importance of building a support network and finding like-minded individuals. We share stories of communities that have come together to promote sustainable fashion.

Inspiring Change
Personal stories have the power to inspire change on a broader scale. This chapter emphasizes the ripple effect of individual actions and how they can

influence others. We encourage readers to share their own stories and become advocates for sustainable fashion.

17

Chapter 17: Call to Action: Redefining Our Fashion Choices

Reflecting on Our Choices
    The final chapter is a call to action, urging readers to reflect on their fashion choices and the impact they have on the planet. We emphasize the importance of being mindful consumers and making informed decisions that align with our values.

Practical Steps for Change
We provide a roadmap for individuals and communities to contribute to the green runway. This includes practical steps such as supporting sustainable brands, reducing consumption, and advocating for ethical practices. We highlight the importance of starting small and building momentum over time.

Collective Responsibility
Achieving a sustainable fashion industry requires collective effort. This chapter discusses the role of consumers, designers, brands, and policymakers in driving change. We emphasize the need for collaboration and the power of collective action.

A Vision for the Future
The chapter concludes with a vision for the future of fashion, where sustainability and ethics are at the core of the industry. We inspire readers

to join the movement and be part of the transformation. Every choice, no matter how small, can make a difference in redefining our fashion landscape.

The Green Runway, Redefining Fashion Through Ecology and Ethical Choices

In a world where fashion often prioritizes speed and profit over ethics and sustainability, "The Green Runway" emerges as a beacon of change. This book delves into the transformative journey of the fashion industry as it redefines itself through ecological mindfulness and ethical choices. From the environmental impact of fast fashion to the rise of eco-fashion pioneers, each chapter explores the innovative strides being made towards a more sustainable future.

Discover the hidden costs of cheap clothing and the environmental damage caused by mass production. Meet the trailblazers who are revolutionizing fashion with sustainable fabrics, ethical production methods, and groundbreaking technologies. Learn how consumer awareness and responsible choices can drive a demand for eco-friendly fashion, and explore the power of activism in pushing the industry towards a more ethical path.

With practical advice on building a sustainable wardrobe, embracing second-hand fashion, and supporting local artisans, "The Green Runway" empowers readers to make informed decisions that align with their values. Through inspiring stories of transformation and personal narratives, this book highlights the collective responsibility and collaborative efforts needed to achieve a fashion industry that respects both people and the planet.

Join us on a journey to redefine fashion, where every choice, no matter how small, can make a difference. "The Green Runway" is a call to action for individuals and communities to contribute to a greener, more ethical fashion landscape. Together, we can walk the path of sustainability and create a future where fashion is a force for good.

www.ingramcontent.com/pod-product-compliance
Lightning Source LLC
LaVergne TN
LVHW010442070526
838199LV00066B/6156